Mathalon Maps

AFRICA

Joanne Randolph

raintree

a Capstone company — publishers for children

Raintree is an imprint of Capstone Global Library
Limited, a company incorporated in England and Wales
having its registered office at 264 Banbury Road, Oxford
OX2 7DY – Registered company number: 6695582

www.raintree.co.uk
myorders@raintree.co.uk

Produced for Raintree by Calcium
Edited by Sarah Eason and Katie Woolley
Designed by Paul Myerscough
Illustrations by Moloko88/Shutterstock
Picture research by Sarah Eason
Production by Victoria Fitzgerald
Originated by Capstone Global Library Ltd © 2016
Printed and bound in China

ISBN 978 1 4747 1592 8
19 18 17 16 15
10 9 8 7 5 4 3 2 1

British Library Cataloguing in Publication Data
A full catalogue record for this book is available from the
British Library.

Acknowledgements
We would like to thank the following for permission
to reproduce photographs: Shutterstock: Bimbom 15tr,
Bzzuspajk 11r, Pocholo Calapre 26r, Hector Conesa
20b, Sam DCruz 17r, 19t, 19b, Chantal de Bruijne 6b,
Pichugin Dmitry 7t, 9t, E2dan 16br, EastVillage Images
13br, EcoPrint 4b, 9b, 29bl, Erichon 12br, 17t, Simon G
23c, Eric Gevaert 24b, 28r, Attila Jandi 21br, Oleksandr
Kalinichenko 7b, Iakov Kalinin 25r, Matej Kastelic 8c,
Daleen Loest 27t, Xavier Marchant 23b, Martchan 5c, 15b,
Mattiaath 13tl, Maggy Meyer 12bl, Andrew Molinaro 14t,
Giulio Napolitano 21t, Noahsu 26l, Anna Omelchenko
16t, 28t, Pecold 5t, Graeme Shannon 14b, Natalia
Sidorova 23t, Mogens Trolle 18, Waj 11l, Andrea Willmore
22bl, 29br, WitR 10t, Vladimir Wrangel 8t, Lara Zanarini 1,
27b, Oleg Znamenskiy 25bl.

Cover photographs reproduced with permission of:
Dreamstime: Teckken Tan (top); Shutterstock: Erichon
(back cover), Pius Lee (bottom).

Every effort has been made to contact copyright holders
of material reproduced in this book. Any omissions will
be rectified in subsequent printings if notice is given to
the publisher.

All the internet addresses (URLs) given in this book
were valid at the time of going to press. However, due
to the dynamic nature of the internet, some addresses
may have changed, or sites may have changed or ceased
to exist since publication. While the author and publisher
regret any inconvenience this may cause readers, no
responsibility for any such changes can be accepted by
either the author or the publisher.

Some words are shown in bold, **like this**. You can
find out what they mean by looking in the glossary.

Contents

Africa

Africa is the second-largest **continent** on Earth. It has one of the world's largest deserts, the longest river and the largest land **mammals**. It is known for its large **savannas**, too. We are about to begin an amazing maths exploration of this continent using our best maths and map skills. Are you ready?

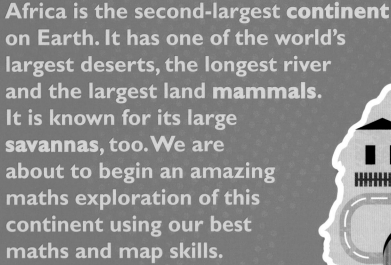

How to use this book

Look for the "Map-a-stat" and "Do the maths" features and complete the maths challenges. Then look at the answers on pages 28 and 29 to see if your calculations are correct.

South Atlantic Ocean

rhino

Africa's regions

Africa's main regions include the Sahara, the Sahel, the Ethiopian Highlands, the savanna, the Swahili coast, the rainforest, the African Great Lakes and Southern Africa. Each of these regions has different features and habitats. They also all have some unique plants and animals living there.

Map-a-stat

Africa has the youngest population of any continent. Around 50 per cent of Africans are aged 25 or younger.

Africa has the second-largest population of any continent, with around 1.1 billion people.

Around 80 people per square km (31 people per sq mile) live in Africa.

Almost two-thirds of Africa's people live in **rural** areas.

Kampala, Uganda

Ethiopian women

Indian Ocean

DO THE MATHS!

Use the information in red in the Map-a-stat box to work out the following challenge. How many of Africa's 1.1 billion people are aged 25 or younger? Here is the equation to help you solve the problem.

1,100,000,000 people × 0.50
(50 per cent) = ? people

Complete the maths challenge, then turn to pages 28—29 to see if your calculation is correct!

Second-largest continent

Africa is the second-largest continent after Asia. If you include its islands, it is 30.3 million sq km (11.7 million sq miles). Algeria is the biggest country in Africa by area, but Nigeria has the biggest population.

Algeria

Ethiopia

Nigeria

Homo sapiens

The earliest human, or *homo sapien*, skeleton was found in Africa. This human lived in Ethiopia around 200,000 years ago. Africa is believed to be the birthplace of the hominids, which are people-like **species** that include **modern** man.

Important remains of early humans have also been found at Olduvai Gorge in Tanzania, Africa.

Map-a-stat

Africa is made up of 54 countries, plus two countries that are disputed, which means that not everyone agrees who should control them. It also has 10 **territories**.

It is believed that the first humans began leaving Africa around 130,000 years ago. These humans went on to populate the rest of the world.

Africa is joined to Asia in the northeast by a strip of land in Egypt called the Isthmus of Suez. The Suez Canal was created in the 1800s to improve trade between Asia and Europe. When it was first built, the canal was 163 km (101 miles) long. Today, it is 193 km (120 miles) long.

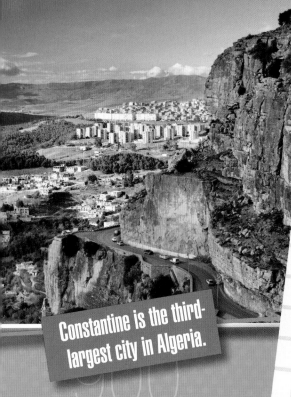

Constantine is the third-largest city in Algeria.

Suez Canal

DO THE MATHS!

Use the information in red in the Map-a-stat box to work out the following challenge. How much longer is the Suez Canal today than it was when it was first built? Use this equation to help you.

$$193 \text{ km} - 163 \text{ km} = ? \text{ km longer}$$

Complete the maths challenge, then turn to pages 28–29 to see if your calculation is correct!

Deserts

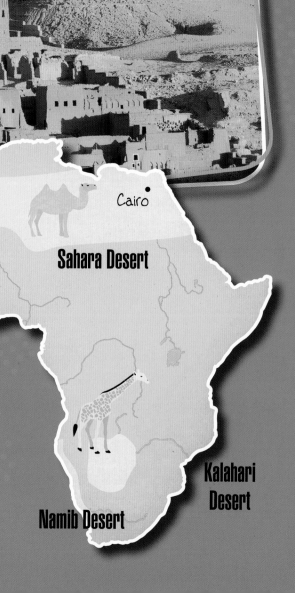

Sahara Desert

Africa is the world's hottest continent and the third-driest. This means it has a lot of deserts. Deserts and **arid** land cover 60 per cent of the continent. The desert areas include the Sahara Desert, the Kalahari Desert and the Namib Desert.

The city of Ait Benhaddou is in north Africa.

Cairo

Sahara Desert

Kalahari Desert

Namib Desert

Sahara Desert

The Sahara Desert is the largest hot desert in the world. Only Antarctica and the Arctic have bigger deserts. It is around 9.3 million sq km (3.6 million sq miles) in area. It covers around one-fourth of the African continent. The northern part of the desert receives around 8 cm (3 in) of rain each year. The southern part receives around 13 cm (5 in). The Sahara Desert is a tough place to live, but many snakes, rodents and scorpions survive there. The fennec fox, jackals and hyenas live in the desert, too. There are also some cities there, such as Cairo in Egypt.

Map-a-stat

The highest point in the Sahara Desert is the **volcano** Emi Koussi, which is 3,415 m (11,204 ft) high.

The Kalahari Desert is a sandy savanna. Its northeastern part is not classified as true desert. This is because it gets too much rain to be called a true desert. The driest parts get between 10-23 cm (4-9 in) of rain each year, while the wetter parts can get up to 51 cm (20 in) of rain every year.

The Namib Desert has been arid or semi-arid for 55 million years, so many scientists consider it to be the oldest desert on Earth.

The Namib Desert has some tall sand dunes. Some are 305 m (1,000 ft) tall. The Sahara Desert has dunes that are around 183 m (600 ft) tall.

Fish River Canyon, Namib Desert

DO THE MATHS!

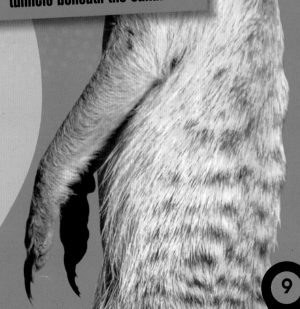

Meerkats make their homes in the Kalahari Desert, digging tunnels beneath the sand.

Use the information in red in the Map-a-stat box to work out the following challenge. How much taller are the Namib Desert's tallest sand dunes than the Sahara Desert's tallest dunes? Use this equation to help you solve the maths challenge.

$$305 \text{ m} - 183 \text{ m} = ? \text{ m}$$

Complete the maths challenge, then turn to pages 28—29 to see if your calculation is correct!

Egypt and the Nile

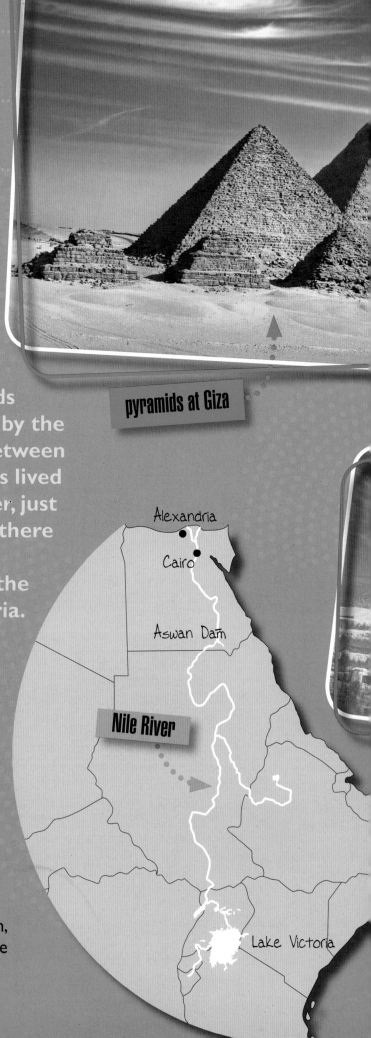

pyramids at Giza

When people think of Africa, some of the first things that may come to mind are the Egyptian pyramids. The pyramids were built as tombs for **royalty** by the ancient Egyptian **civilization** between 2686–1650 BC. Ancient Egyptians lived along the banks of the Nile River, just as modern Egyptians do. Today, there are 86.9 million people living in Egypt. The two largest cities in the country are Cairo and Alexandria.

The Nile River

At around 6,650 km (4,132 miles) long, the Nile River is the longest river in the world. It flows through 10 countries. Surrounding the Nile are some areas of rich farmland. Much of the surrounding land is part of the Sahara Desert. A long time ago, the Nile River would **flood** regularly. This helped spread **fertile** deposits across the land surrounding the river, which helped plants grow. The Nile no longer floods land below the Aswan Dam, which was built in 1970. This has changed the land and it is not as farmable as it once was.

Alexandria

Cairo

Aswan Dam

Nile River

Lake Victoria

Map-a-stat

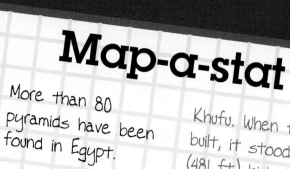

More than 80 pyramids have been found in Egypt.

The largest pyramid in Egypt is the Great Pyramid of Giza, also known as the Pyramid of Khufu. When first built, it stood 147 m (481 ft.) high, but is now only 137 m (451 ft.) high. Its base is 230 m (756 ft.) long on each of its four sides.

A sphinx guards the Pyramid of Khufu. Khufu was a pharaoh, or king, of Egypt a long time ago.

Cairo is the capital of Egypt and the second-largest city in Africa.

DO THE MATHS!

Use the information in red in the Map-a-stat box to work out the following challenge. What is the perimeter of the base of the Great Pyramid of Giza? Use this equation to help you.

$$230 + 230 + 230 + 230 = ?\text{ m in perimeter}$$

Complete the maths challenge, then turn to pages 28—29 to see if your calculation is correct!

Savannas

Savannas are **grassland biomes**. In Africa, they cover a wide area that includes land from 28 countries. Like deserts, savannas in Africa tend to be dry but they receive enough rainfall to support more plant and animal life than deserts.

lion

The Serengeti Plain

The Serengeti Plain has many different habitats, including savannas, woodlands and open grasslands. Many animals you think of when you picture Africa live in the Serengeti. It has many mammal species, including zebras, wildebeest, elephants, giraffes, cheetahs and lions. The plain is famous for the Great Migration of wildebeest and zebras. In spring, they **migrate** north to fertile **grazing** lands, then in Autumn, they head back to the southern grasslands.

Animals graze on the savanna in Kenya.

Map-a-stat

Up to 400,000 zebras and 1.5 million wildebeest migrate from south to north and back again each year. It is a tough trip. Around 250,000 wildebeest die during the journey back south. They die from hunger, thirst, exhaustion and from being hunted by lions, cheetahs and crocodiles.

Savannas cover about 50 per cent of Africa's land.

The savannas of Africa cover 13 million sq km (5 million sq miles) of its total area, which is 30.3 million sq km (11.7 million sq miles).

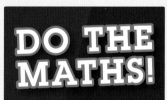

Giraffes make their homes on the Serengeti Plain and other African savannas.

The Great Migration

DO THE MATHS!

Use the information in red in the Map-a-stat box to work out the following challenge. If 250,000 of the 1.5 million wildebeest die during the Great Migration, how many wildebeest survive? Here is the equation to help you solve the problem.

1,500,000 wildebeest - 250,000 wildebeest = ? wildebeest

Complete the maths challenge, then turn to pages 28—29 to see if your calculation is correct!

Mountains

Most people picture deserts and grasslands when they think of Africa. However, Africa has many mountain ranges. Ethiopia has 50 per cent of Africa's highest mountains. Tanzania is home to several ranges, including the Mahale Mountains and the Udzungwa Mountains. It is also home to Africa's tallest mountain, Mount Kilimanjaro, which is 5,895 m (19,340 ft.) high.

chimpanzee

The Ethiopian Highlands

There are two main ranges that make up the Ethiopian Highlands. These are the Simien and Bale ranges. The Great Rift Valley, which you will read more about later, lies between these ranges. Ethiopians grow coffee and a grain, called teff, on the slopes of the mountains. Many animals make their homes in these ranges, too. Some of them include the gelada **baboon**, the walia **ibex** and the Ethiopian wolf.

Simien Mountains

Ethiopia

Mount Kilimanjaro

Bale Mountains

Mount Kilimanjaro is Africa's highest mountain.

Tanzania

Udzungwa Mountains

Mahale Mountains

Map-a-stat

The Mahale Mountains are home to some of the last remaining wild chimpanzees. There is a population of 900 there.

The **Ethiopian wolf** is a symbol of Ethiopia. Sadly, it is almost **extinct** with only about 440 wolves remaining. The wolves tend to travel in packs of around six adults.

The Udzungwa Mountains are home to more than 400 species of birds. They also have a beautiful waterfall, called the Sanje, which falls 170 m. (558 ft.).

the Sanje

People live in traditional ways in the Ethiopian Highlands.

DO THE MATHS!

Use the information in red in the Map-a-stat box to work out the following challenge. If there are 440 Ethiopian wolves and they tend to travel in packs of six adults, how many packs of wolves are there in the Highlands? You will need to round up your answer. Here is the equation to help you solve the problem.

440 wolves ÷ 6 adult wolves per pack = ? packs

Complete the maths challenge, then turn to pages 28—29 to see if your calculation is correct!

Lakes

Africa has major lakes, called the African Great Lakes. These lakes were created when Earth's shifting **plates** caused deep cracks to form in Africa's **crust**. Some of the lakes are Lake Albert, Lake Edward, Lake Kivu, Lake Malawi, Lake Tanganyika, Lake Turkana and Lake Victoria. Many African plants and animals depend on these lakes to provide them with the water they need to live.

These hippos live in Lake Naivasha in Kenya.

Lake Victoria

Lake Victoria is Africa's largest lake and has an area of 69,484 sq km (26,828 sq miles). By area, it is the second-largest freshwater lake in the world, after Lake Superior in the United States. Lake Victoria is one of the main sources of the Nile River. The countries Uganda, Kenya and Tanzania border the lake.

Victoria Falls is 1,700 m (5,500 ft.) wide.

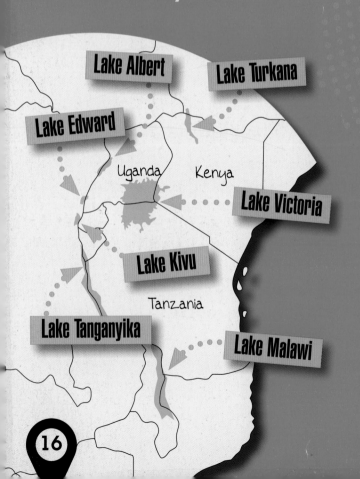

Lake Albert
Lake Turkana
Lake Edward
Uganda
Kenya
Lake Victoria
Lake Kivu
Tanzania
Lake Tanganyika
Lake Malawi

Map-a-stat

Lake Victoria has a shoreline of more than 3,220 km (2,000 miles).

Lake Tanganyika is the world's second-largest freshwater lake by volume. It is also the second-deepest after Lake Baikal in Siberia. Its maximum depth is 1,436 m (4,710 ft).

Lake Tanganyika's shoreline is 1,838 km (1,142 miles) long.

These fishermen are beginning their day at Lake Malawi.

Lake Nukuru

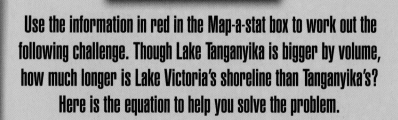

DO THE MATHS!

Use the information in red in the Map-a-stat box to work out the following challenge. Though Lake Tanganyika is bigger by volume, how much longer is Lake Victoria's shoreline than Tanganyika's? Here is the equation to help you solve the problem.

$$3{,}220 \text{ km} - 1{,}838 \text{ km} = ? \text{ km longer}$$

Complete the maths challenge, then turn to pages 28—29 to see if your calculation is correct!

The Great Rift Valley

The East African Rift System runs from Jordan to Mozambique, covering a distance of 6,400 km (4,000 miles). A rift is a place where parts of Earth's crust are moving away from each other. Part of the East African Rift System is the Great Rift Valley in Africa.

Home, burning home?

The Great Rift Valley is a habitat for many plants and animals, including elephants and hippos. Most of these plants and animals live on the grasslands, by rivers or on the slopes of mountains. There is one unlikely habitat in the valley, though. The valley has some lakes that are full of a **chemical** called sodium carbonate. This burns most living things. However, the lesser flamingo manages to wade in the waters without being harmed. It eats the tiny **algae** that live in the lakes. Thousands of flamingos feed in the Great Rift Valley's many lakes.

Flamingos feed at Lake Nakuru in Kenya.

Great Rift Valley

Indian Ocean

Map-a-stat

If the two African plates that helped form the Great Rift Valley keep moving at their current rate, it will take 10 million years for a new **landmass** to break off.

The Great Rift Valley's highest point is 1,830 m (6,000 ft) above sea level. The lowest point in Africa is Lake Assal, which is 157 m (515 ft) below sea level.

Around 4 million flamingos make their home in the Great Rift Valley's lakes.

The Great Rift Valley in Kenya

Baboons make their home in the Great Rift Valley.

DO THE MATHS!

Use the information in red in the Map-a-stat box to work out the following challenge. If you were to walk to the highest point of the Great Rift Valley at a rate of 1.2 metres per minute, how many minutes would it take you to reach the top? Here is the equation to help you solve the problem.

$$1{,}830 \text{ m} \div 1.2 \text{ m per minute} = ? \text{ minutes}$$

Complete the maths challenge, then turn to pages 28–29 to see if your calculation is correct!

The Sahel

Between the Sahara Desert and the savanna, there is a special habitat called the Sahel. It is semi-arid and stretches from the Atlantic Ocean to Sudan. The Sahel area is found in a number of regions, including parts of the Gambia, Senegal, Mauritania, Mali, Niger, Nigeria, Sudan, South Sudan, Burkina Faso and Eritrea. It used to be home to many grazing herds of gazelle and **oryx**. Hunting and competition with livestock have pushed most of these animals towards extinction.

Red Sea

the Sahel

Atlantic Ocean

Women in Burkina Faso, in the Sahel region, head to work.

Climate

Like the rest of the Sahara Desert, the Sahel is very dry. It is said to have a semi-arid **climate**, though, because it does have a rainy season. The southern part of the Sahel gets between 50–60 cm (20–24 in) of rain each year. The middle area gets around 18 cm (7 in) of rain per year. The northern part of the Sahel gets between 10–20 cm (4–8 in) of rain each year.

Map-a-stat

Stretching from the Atlantic Ocean to the Red Sea, the Sahel stretches 3,862 km (2,400 miles) across. The distance from the Atlantic Ocean to the Pacific Ocean in the United States is about 4,828 km (3,000 miles).

Between 1972 and 1984, 100,000 people in the Sahel died due to **drought**.

Tough plants, such as the acacia and baobab tree, grow in the Sahel. The baobab tree can have a trunk up to 9 m (30 ft.) in diameter, and can be 18 m (159 ft.) tall.

This is an arid area of the Sahel in Niger.

A woman carries her son to the market in Mali.

DO THE MATHS!

Use the information in red in the Map-a-stat box to work out the following challenge. How much further is it from coast to coast in the United States than it is in the Sahel? Here is the equation to help you solve the problem.

$$4{,}828 \text{ km} - 3{,}862 \text{ km} = ? \text{ km longer}$$

Complete the maths challenge, then turn to pages 28—29 to see if your calculation is correct!

Coasts

Africa has a lot of coasts. Most of Africa's largest cities are in the coastal areas. Of the mainland countries with coasts, the mainland country with the largest stretch of coast is Somalia, with 3,025 km (1,880 miles) along the Indian Ocean. The country that has the least amount of shoreline is Democratic Republic of Congo, with only 37 km (23 miles) of coast.

Mediterranean Sea

Red Sea

Nigeria

Somalia

Atlantic Ocean

Democratic Republic of Congo

Indian Ocean

Cape Town is a large city in South Africa.

Nigeria

Nigeria is one of Africa's coastal countries. It is not the largest African country by area. However, it has the largest population and **economy**. More than 177 million people live in Nigeria. Its biggest industry is oil, but it also has thriving **telecommunications** and financial businesses.

Monastir, Tunisia, sits on the Mediterranean Sea.

Map-a-stat

Though Africa is the second-largest continent and it has 26,000 km (16,000 miles) of coastline, it does not have a lot of inlets, or indents, in its coast. This means that it has less coastal area than the much smaller European continent.

Africa's coasts have a rich **resource** of fish and other ocean life. These fish provide food and employment for many Africans. In fact, around 10 million people in Africa work for **fisheries**.

Maputo, the capital of Mozambique, lies on the Indian Ocean.

Lagos, Nigeria, is the largest city in Nigeria and an important port.

DO THE MATHS!

Use the information in red in the Map-a-stat box to work out the following challenge. If you were in a boat sailing around Africa's coast at 16 km per hour, how long would it take you to circle the coast? Here is the equation to help you solve the problem.

$$26,000 \text{ km} \div 16 \text{ km per hour} = ? \text{ hours}$$

Complete the maths challenge, then turn to pages 28—29 to see if your calculation is correct!

Islands

Seychelles

Indian Ocean

Madagascar

Mauritius

Africa has many islands in the waters surrounding the continent. Most of the islands are small, and are less than 1,994 sq km (770 sq miles). The only island considered large is Madagascar. Seychelles is a country made up of many islands, as are Comoros and Cape Verde. Mauritius is a well-known African island.

Madagascar

Madagascar is Africa's largest island. It is also the fourth-largest island in the world. Many unique and interesting animals make their home on Madagascar. More than 23 million people do, too. The island has many different habitats, from deserts to fertile plateaus used for growing rice and other crops. It also has hot, steamy rainforests.

Lemurs are mainly found on Madagascar.

Map-a-stat

Around 70 per cent of Madagascar's wildlife is found nowhere else on Earth.

There are around 103 species of lemurs living on Madagascar.

Seychelles is made up of 115 islands.

Madagascar has around 258 bird species, and around 115 of them are found only on the island.

Most of Africa's islands are in the Indian Ocean but there are a few in the Atlantic Ocean, too.

Many people visit Seychelles to enjoy its beautiful beaches.

Mauritius is a tropical island ringed by mountains.

DO THE MATHS!

Use the information in red in the Map-a-stat box to work out the following challenge. If there are 115 species of birds in Madagascar that are found nowhere else on Earth, how many of its 258 bird species can be found in other places? Here is the equation to help you solve the problem.

258 species - 115 species = ? bird species that also live on other continents

Complete the maths challenge, then turn to pages 28—29 to see if your calculation is correct!

An amazing continent

Africa is an amazing continent. It covers around one-fifth of the planet's land area and has 15 per cent of Earth's population. As the "cradle of humanity", it is the place where modern humans began. Africa also has some of the most fascinating animals in the world, with gorillas, hippos, lions, cheetahs, hyenas, lemurs and many more.

gorilla

Exploration

Vasco da Gama sailed around the Cape of Good Hope in South Africa.

Africa gave birth to the first humans, and then some of those humans left to explore and settle in new lands. That itch for discovery stayed with humans. In the 1400s, Europeans, who were looking for resources and **trade routes**, began to further explore the coasts of Africa. The voyage led by Vasco da Gama from 1498–1499 was the first to sail all the way around the southern tip of Africa to reach India. The trip made it easier to trade with Africa, Asian countries and Pacific Islands, which had spices and other goods Europeans wanted. Today, Africa still has goods that are very valuable, especially oil.

Map-a-stat

Vasco da Gama's first voyage from Portugal around the Cape of Good Hope to India and back took two years. In that time, he sailed 38,600 km (24,000 miles) and spent 300 days at sea.

Africa has one of the largest mineral industries in the world, with 57 per cent of the world's cobalt, 39 per cent of its manganese and 46 per cent of its natural diamonds, to name just a few.

African elephants are the largest land mammals. These huge animals stand 3.4 m (11 ft.) tall at the shoulder and can be up to 7.3 m (24 ft.) long.

Many rural parts of Africa rely on solar panels for energy.

elephant

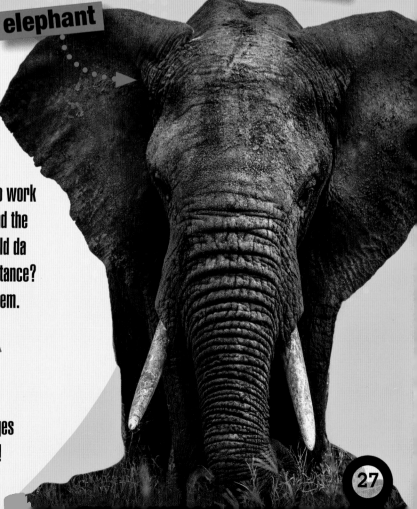

DO THE MATHS!

Use the information in red in the Map-a-stat box to work out the following challenge. If the distance around the equator is 40,074 km, how many more km would da Gama's crew have needed to sail to match this distance? Here is the equation to help you solve the problem.

$$40,074 \text{ km} - 38,600 \text{ km} = ? \text{ km}$$

Complete the maths challenge, then turn to pages 28—29 to see if your calculation is correct!

Maths challenge answers

You have made it through the mathalon! How did your maths skills measure up? Check your answers below.

Page 5

$1,100,000,000 \text{ people} \times 0.50$
$= 550,000,000 \text{ people}$

Page 7

$193 \text{ km} - 163 \text{ km}$
$= 30 \text{ km longer}$

Page 9

$305 \text{ m} - 183 \text{ m}$
$= 122 \text{ m}$

Page 11

$230 + 230 + 230 + 230$
$= 920 \text{ m in perimeter}$

Page 13

$1,500,000 \text{ wildebeest} - 250,000 \text{ wildebeest}$
$= 1,250,000 \text{ wildebeest}$

Page 15

440 wolves ÷ 6 adult wolves per pack
= about 73 packs

Page 17

3,220 km – 1,838 km = 1,382 km longer

Page 19

1,830 m ÷ 1.2 m per minute = 1,525 minutes

Page 21

4,828 km – 3,862 km = 966 km longer

Page 23

26,000 km ÷ 16 km per hour
= 1,625 hours

Page 25

258 species – 115 species
= 143 bird species that also
live on other continents

Page 27

40,074 km – 38,600 km
= 1,474 km

DO THE MATHS!

Glossary

algae tiny plant-like organisms that live in water

arid very hot and dry

baboon type of large monkey with a snout like a dog's nose

biome large area of land with similar plants and animals

chemical substance that is used in or produced by a chemical process

civilization people who have an organized society

climate weather conditions in a certain area

continent one of Earth's seven large landmasses

crust outer, or top, layer of a planet

drought long period of time in which an area receives little or no rain

economy system of how money is made and used within a particular region or country

equator imaginary line around the middle of Earth

extinct no longer existing

fertile describes ground that is rich and able to produce crops and other plants

fishery company that makes money from catching and selling fish

flood when water spills out of a river and on to the surrounding land

grassland large area of land covered by grass

grazing eating grass

habitat surrounding area where animals or plants naturally live

hyena carnivore that lives in Africa and Asia and eats the remains of dead animals

ibex type of wild goat found in the mountains of Europe, Asia and Africa

jackal dog-like wild animal found in Africa, Europe and Asia

landmass huge area of land

mammal animal that has warm blood and often fur. Most mammals give birth to live young and feed their babies with milk from their bodies.

migrate move from one habitat or location to another

modern in recent history, not ancient

oryx type of antelope

plateau large, flat area that is at higher altitude than the surrounding region

plate moving piece of Earth's crust, the top layer of Earth

resource something that people need to live, such as fuel or food

royalty kings, queens, princes, princesses and anyone related to a royal family

rural area that does not have towns or cities

savanna area of grassland with few trees or bushes

species single kind of living thing. All people are one species.

telecommunication science and technology of communication

territory particular area of land that belongs to and is controlled by a country

trade route route along which people bought and sold goods

volcano opening in Earth's crust through which ash, gases and melted rock are forced out

Find out more

Books

Africa (Introducing Continents), Chris Oxlade
(Raintree, 2014)

Kenya (Countries in Our World), Alison Brownlie Bojang
(Franklin Watts, 2013)

Letters to Africa, UCLan
(UCLan Publishing, 2010)

Nile (River Adventures), Paul Manning
(Franklin Watts, 2014)

South Africa (Unpacked), Clive Gifford
(Wayland, 2015)

Websites

Learn more about Africa and its geography at:
www.ducksters.com/geography/africa.php

Take a look at some more maps of Africa at:
www.enchantedlearning.com/school/Africa/Africamap.shtml

Find out more about children's lives in Africa at:
www.our-africa.org

Index